The Young Persons' Way to the Guitar

Segovia with the Author

THE
YOUNG PERSONS'
WAY TO THE
GUITAR

by

JOHN W. DUARTE

FOR THE TEACHER

NOVELLO

ABOUT THE GUITAR

There are strong links between the guitar and Spain, such as its use in *Flamenco*, Spanish folk-music, but there is no reason to believe that the instrument was finally developed in that country. It is quite inappropriate to call it the 'Spanish' guitar, though many people do so. Many of the details of the guitar as we now know it were arrived at, about 100 years ago, by a Spaniard, but long before that time there were excellent guitars made in many countries. For that matter, the modern violin was developed by Italian craftsmen, but no one ever calls it the 'Italian' violin—not even the Italians! Today, the best guitar makers, players, and composers, come from very many countries. Whatever its history may be, the guitar is now international.

It would be nice and simple if we could just call it 'the guitar', as we speak of 'the violin' or 'the flute', but in the last century there have been so many adaptations of the guitar to suit it to different purposes, that the word 'guitar' now means different things to different people. The instrument, in its most aristocratic and oldest form, now has several names to distinguish it:

Concert guitar: Little used, and of little value since all kinds of guitar are used in all kinds of concert!

Fingerstyle guitar: Another name of little value. This kind of guitar *is* played with the fingers of the right hand, but so too are some other kinds.

Classic guitar: The most-used and best name. It does not mean that the instrument is used only for 'classical' music; it refers to the highly-developed and refined design of the instrument itself, which gives it a long-lasting value.

Maybe one day the other kinds of guitar will be given new names—they are, after all, quite different instruments—and then we can once more call the classic instrument quite simply 'the guitar', without risk of being misunderstood.

OTHER KINDS OF GUITAR

The *Flamenco guitar* is very similar to the classic guitar but it is built much more lightly; you would know the difference if you picked them both up. It also has a

Flamenco guitar[1]

plate, usually made of plastic, to protect its front when the player strikes it like a drum with his right hand, as he often does in this kind of music. The classic guitar can be used for Flamenco music but it is not entirely successful.

The *plectrum guitar* was developed early in this century to give a louder sound, needed in the playing of some kinds of popular music. It has steel strings instead of

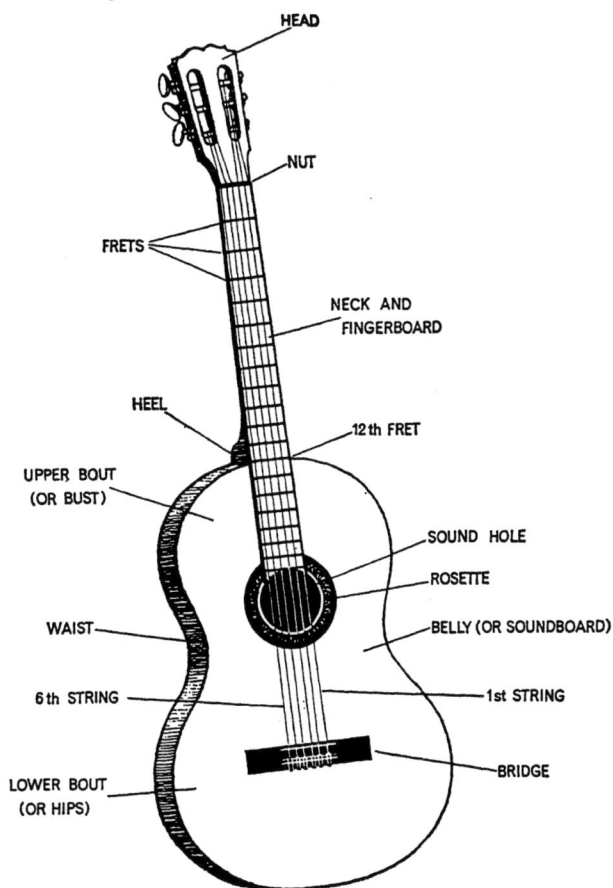

Main parts of the classic guitar

[1] Spanish Guitar Centre, Bristol

the gut or nylon ones of the classic guitar, it is constructed very strongly to withstand these strings, and it is

Plectrum (acoustic) guitar[2]

played with a plectrum (a piece of hard shell or plastic held in the right hand*). This kind of guitar is shaped differently and it is still widely used.

The *electric guitar* was first developed in the 1930s. Even the plectrum guitar was not really loud enough to stand alongside the other instruments of popular music as a solo instrument; the electrically-amplified guitar is well able to do this. The sound of an electrically-amplified guitar now depends very little, if at all, on the shape and size of the instrument: it is determined by the electrical side of the equipment. Electric guitars are now made, therefore, in all shapes and sizes; many are hardly recognizable as guitars, and many others are made in odd shapes solely to attract attention—like ladies' hats at Ascot.

There are many other varieties of guitar, including the Hawaiian guitar—which is not really a guitar at all. Each has its use and each is difficult to play, in its

---

* The plectrum is not a modern innovation. It has been used often in the history of music. A wire-strung, plectrum-played guitar with five strings did exist in England and was popular in the eighteenth century.

[2] Mairants Musicentre Ltd, Rathbone Place, London W1

own way. They do not really compete with one another. The classic guitar is the most versatile of all and it can play the most worthwhile music; it is the one that can best serve you as a friend for the rest of your life.

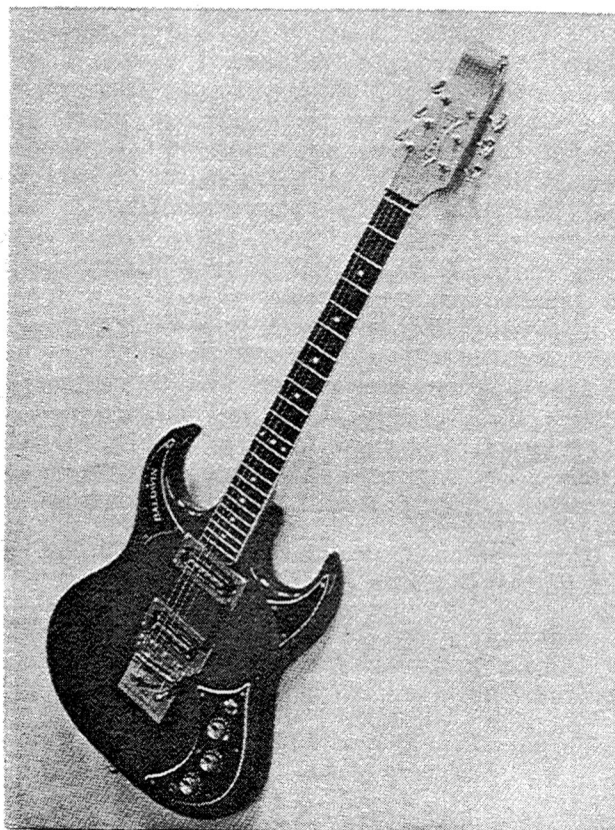

Electric guitar[3]

IMPORTANT PEOPLE

These are perhaps the most remarkable of the many important people in the history of the guitar:

Fernando Sor (1778-1839)

A very great Spanish player who contributed very considerably to the popularity and status of the guitar by his compositions and his concerts all over Europe; he came to England with much success in 1809. Sor also developed the use of the third finger of the right hand, previously much less important than the first and second.

Other important guitarist-composers of the same period, whose names you will often meet, include Fernando Carulli (1770-1841), Mauro Giuliani (1780-1829), Dionisio Aguado (1784-1849), and Matteo Carcassi (1792-1853).

Antonio Torres (1817-1892)

A Spanish craftsman who developed the constructional details and dimensions of the guitar that still form the basis of modern manufacture, even though they are not rigidly adhered to. Before Torres there was nothing in the

---

[3] Baldwin Burns Ltd, Buckhurst Hill, Essex

nature of a 'standard'. He may be regarded as the 'father' of the present-day guitar.

Francisco Tárrega (1854-1909)

Another great Spanish player who further developed the technique of playing and who was a modest composer. His greatest contribution was in demonstrating how effectively music written for the pianoforte and other instruments could be arranged for the guitar. He was highly thought of by some famous composers (not guitarists) of his day; many were his friends. Tárrega did little to popularize the guitar with the general public.

Andres Segovia (born 1893)

It is almost impossible to exaggerate the importance of this 'father figure' of the guitar—probably the greatest guitarist in history. Modern classic guitar technique is based on his innovations and on the way in which he has built on the work of his predecessors. In almost seventy years of concert-giving he has travelled many times around the world, played in every country, made very many gramophone records, arranged a great deal of music, and inspired numerous composers everywhere to write for the guitar. Almost single-handed he has brought the guitar to its present state of world-wide popularity, making it possible for the new wave of great players to find a ready-made audience. He has been responsible for the fact that many academies and colleges of music now include the guitar in their curricula. None of this would have been achieved if he had not also been a very fine musician and one of the great interpreters of music.

Albert Augustine

Before Albert Augustine, guitar strings were made from gut or wire-wound silk. They were unreliable, short-lived, and expensive It was Augustine who first developed, in the late 1940s, guitar strings made from nylon. No one without experience of the old strings can possibly appreciate the importance of what Albert Augustine did.

There are now many fine guitarists giving concerts and you should lose no opportunity of hearing them. The best of these 'new-wave' players are Julian Bream (English), John Williams (Australian, now British), and Alirio Diaz (Venezuelan). These artists show what a magnificent and exciting instrument the guitar can be, and you might even be lucky enough to hear Segovia, who still comes to England at least once a year.

Photograph by Sandra Lousada

Reproduced by permission of Whitecross Studio Ltd.

JULIAN BREAM

Section One

GETTING STARTED

At the beginning of this section you will find a number of 'Ladders'. Each of these consists of a few different notes played along one string of the guitar. Just as you can climb up and down a wooden or metal ladder and, the higher you climb, the more you can see of your surroundings, so you will first learn to use one short ladder and then you will add others, as extensions. The longer ladder that they form will make it possible for you to reach more and more music. Your teacher will tell you how to climb up and down these ladders and how to use them. We hope you will enjoy the 'views' you will get as you climb them.

Ladders

Count regularly and steadily:
One-two, for a half-note
One-two-three-four, for a whole-note.

19628

2

D

String ④
Fret Finger: 0 2 3 2 0 2 8 2 0

C and D combined

String ④ ③ ④
Fret Finger: 0 2 3 0 2 0 8 2 0

A, B, C and D combined

String ④ ③ ② ①
Fret Finger: 0 2 3 0 2 0 1 3 0 1

② ③ ④
3 1 0 3 1 0 2 0 3 2 0

E

String ⑤
Fret Finger: 0 2 3 2 0 2 3 2 0

Scale of C

String ⑤ ④ ③ ② ③ ④ ⑤
Fret Finger: 3 0 2 3 0 2 0 1 0 2 0 3 2 0 3

D and E combined

String ⑤ ④ ⑤
Fret Finger: 0 2 3 0 2 3 2 0 3 2 0

A, B, C, D and E combined

String ⑤ ④ ③ ② ①
Fret Finger: 0 2 3 0 2 3 0 2 0 1 3 0 1 3

② ③ ④ ⑤
1 0 3 1 0 2 0 3 2 0 3 2 0

19628

String
F
Fret
Finger
String
E and F combined
Fret
Finger
String
All ladders from A to F joined
Fret
Finger
Scale of G

My First Tune

You need only the notes from Ladder A:

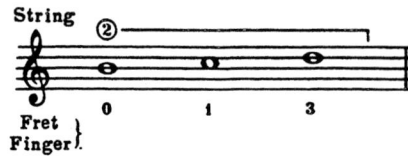

A whole-note (a semibreve) ○ lasts for a steady count of four

A half-note (a minim) ♩ lasts for only two beats

Count out aloud to yourself when practising alone. When you are play-ing with the other guitar it will help by doing the counting for you: it has one note for each beat. Hold each note down and do not change or let it go until it has been counted out in full.

John W. Duarte

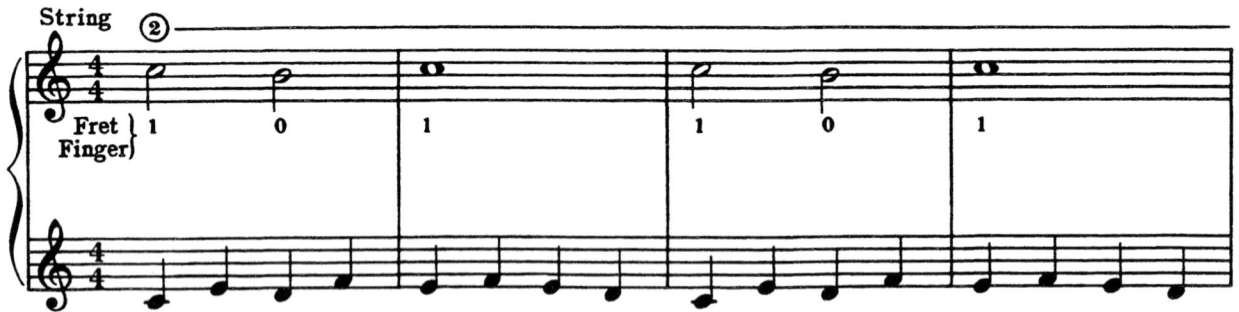

Our New Car

The time is the same as in the last piece, 4/4, and you are still using the same note-values: whole-notes (count four beats) and half-notes (count two beats). The second guitar still counts the beats for you by playing a note on each beat.

What's new?

You need the notes from Ladder A as before but now you need those for Ladder B too:

When you change from one string to the next, make sure you strike the *right* string, it is easy to make a mistake in this way.

John W. Duarte

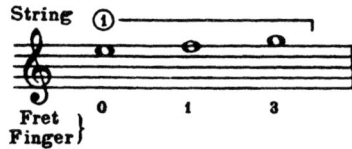

The Cuckoo

What's new?

This piece is in ¾ time, with three beats (counts) to the bar. There are no whole-notes but there are half-notes (two beats) as before; there are also quarter-notes which take a count of only one:

one-two | one

Again, the second guitar plays one note to each beat and does the counting for you but, when you are playing alone, count aloud to yourself like this:

three | one-two | three | one-two | three | one | two | three | *etc.*

John W. Duarte

Going for a Pony Ride

When you lift and put down your finger repeatedly on a string, as you do in the first two bars, be careful to do it exactly in time with the counting, not ahead or behind it!

What's new?

The long curved lines over the staff mean that you play all the notes under each one as though they all belonged together, as though they were a sentence that you were speaking all on one breath.

There are two little dashes like this ‖ above the staff in two places. These mean that at that place you pause for a moment, like taking a quick breath before you go on talking.

John W. Duarte

On the Bridge at Avignon

Sur le Pont D'Avignon

What's new?

The notes from both Ladders A and B are needed, also the lower of the two notes in the very short Ladder C:

You now have to cross not only back and forth between the first and second strings, but also between the second and third strings in the same way. Be twice as careful then to strike the right string when you have to change.

French folk song

Bugle and Drum

There is more changing from string to string than before, so you must watch *very* carefully. It is a little harder than the last piece.

What's new?

Try to follow the suggestions about how loud you play the part; 'quite loudly' and 'very loudly'. Strike the strings as hard as you can in the places marked 'very loudly', without making them rattle, and not quite so strongly in the other places.

John W. Duarte

In the Moonlight

Au Clair de la Lune

What's new?

One more note, to complete the short Ladder C:

Now you have used all the notes on the first three ladders.

French nursery song

Bobby Shaftoe

What's new?

The last note of the first bar is on the same fret (but not the same string) as the one before it. To avoid jerking your first finger from one string to the other, you use the second finger for the second note and then return the hand to its usual position. This happens once more, four bars later.

My Bonny

What's new?

There are half- and quarter-notes as before but there are also *dotted* half-notes. The dot makes the half-note half as long again so that it takes a count not of two, but of three, lasting for a whole bar in $^3/_4$ time (three beats *i.e.* two beats and one for the dot).

$$\text{d.} \quad = \quad \text{d} \quad + \quad \text{d}$$
one - two / three

In the third and fourth complete bars there are two E's joined by a curved line. This line is a TIE or BIND, and it means that you strike only the first of the two notes but hold it for the full value of both:

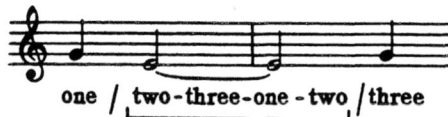

one / two-three-one-two / three

The E is held then for a total of four beats (two and two). In bars 7 and 8 the two D's are held for five beats altogether (three and two), and in bars 15 and 16 the two C's are held for six beats altogether (three and three):

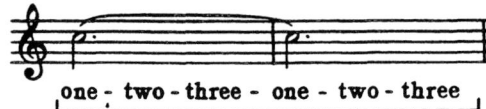

one-two-three-one-two / three   one - two - three - one - two - three

One new note, from Ladder D:

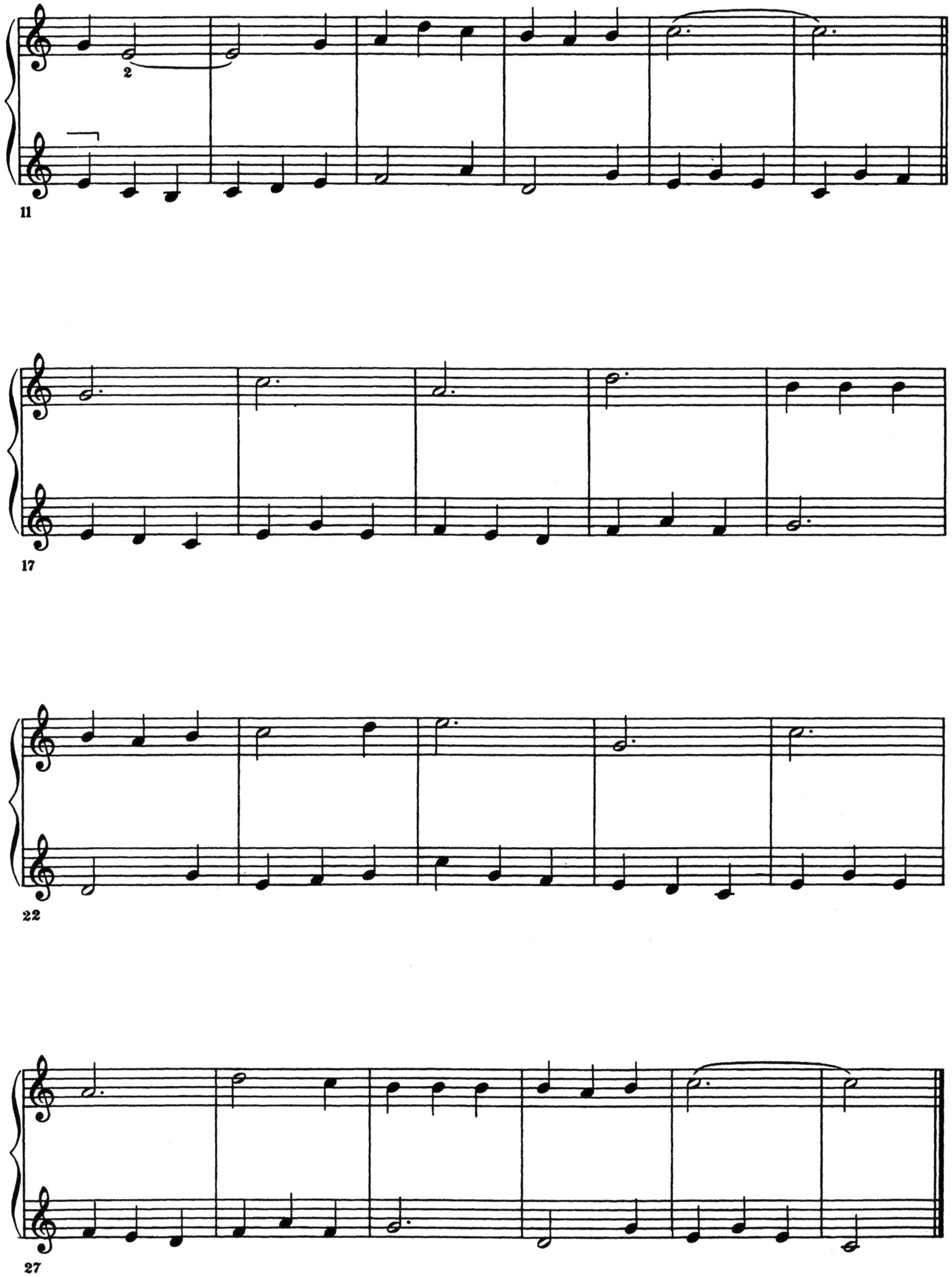
2
11
17
22
27

Conversation

The important thing is to make the parts fit together; for this you will have to count very carefully and listen to the other part. Watch the long curved lines over the staff and play your 'sentences' (some are very short remarks !) as you did in *Going for a Pony Ride*. Try also to follow the directions about playing loudly and softly.

What's new?

One more note from Ladder D:

John W. Duarte

19628

O Come All Ye Faithful

There is nothing new except that at bar 13 you have two bars on your own before the other guitar joins you. You will recognise the place easily from the times you have heard or sung the tune at Christmas. Count carefully and *do not hurry*.

The Grand Old Duke of York

What's new?

This piece has dotted half-notes (as in *My Bonny*), and quarter notes. For the first time it has eighth-notes. There are two of these to each beat and you count the second one as 'and', thus:

one - and

The counting of the sixth bar would look this way:

one / two-and / three / four-and

Each pair of eighth-notes has the same note twice.

Of course, the 'one, two, three, four' come evenly and steadily just as they have always done before; the 'and's are squeezed in between without upsetting the counting.

Polly Wolly Doodle

There are no new things about this piece but there are more eighth-notes than in the last piece. Some of the pairs of eighth-notes are made up of two different notes (like the very first pair in the whole piece). In bars **7** and **15** (first note in each) you have to use two different fingers at the same fret on two strings; to avoid having to jerk the third finger from the last note (D) of the previous bars, on the second string, to the first string, the fourth finger is used.

19628

Ship Ahoy!

What's new?

Some notes have little 'arrow heads' > and these are called ACCENTS.
The notes marked like this should be played more strongly than the others;
they are to be accented.

John W. Duarte

19628

The Ash Grove

There is nothing new here, but the groups of eighth-notes are mostly longer than before. The only groups of four that you have had before have been mainly on one note, but these are of four different notes.

Waltz

Only old friends in this piece, but there are more groups of eighth-notes
than before and they all move from note to note.

John W. Duarte

Lavender Blue

What's new?

All the tunes you have played so far finish on the note C. Many of them started on this note too. You have seen how the notes you have used can be arranged in a different kind of ladder, called the 'scale of C'. All the pieces you have played have been in the key of C. This tune starts and finishes on the note G and is in the KEY OF G. The sharp sign (♯) at the beginning of each staff between the clef and the time-signature, also tells you that the key is G. It means that you must play *every* F in the piece as though it had a sharp sign in front of it. The sharp sign, used in this way, is called a KEY-SIGNATURE and it announces the key just as the time-signature announces the kind of time (³/₄ or ⁴/₄ for instance). There is no F in the tune (in either part) so for the moment you do not have to worry about playing your F's sharp! Do notice though that the tune comes to rest on G just as the previous ones did on C.

Baa, Baa Black Sheep

What's new?

The sharp sign just after the first clef tells you that the tune is in the key of G. There is only one F in the tune and it must, as you know now, be played sharp; that means that it is played at the second fret on the first string. The sharp is not shown against the F; you must keep it in your mind from the moment you see the key-signature. We have then one new note:

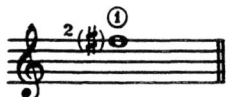

The changes from one string to the next in the eighth-notes in the last bar are a little harder than they look. Be careful!

John Peel

Another piece in the key of G but this time with *three* F sharps.

What's new?

Twice, in bars 7 and 15, you must play the F sharp below the one you first learned:

Again the note does not have a sharp in front of it, but it must be played with one, as the key-signature tells you. The key-signature shows a sharp on the top F only but the sharp is meant to be added to *every* F, whether high or low, and even other F's that you do not yet know!

Follow Me!

What's new?

You have the first bar all to yourself and after that you must concentrate on what *you* are doing. Stick to your guns! What you play will be played again exactly, one octave lower, *one bar later;* the other guitar really *does* follow you. Don't let it put you off. This kind of music is called a CANON: one part is just like the other, but it starts later.

The first two notes of the last bar are another example of two different fingers being used for notes at the same fret but on different strings; this time they are the second and third fingers.

John W. Duarte

The Chase

The previous piece was a canon, with one part imitating the other as it followed on; not only is this fun, it helps you too to hold your own. This piece is also a canon and, as one part 'chases' the other, you should learn to play it as briskly as you can.

John W. Duarte

Cowboys

What's new?

There is one new note (see bar 11)

The ♯ sign, used in this way, written before the note, does not belong to the key-signature but is called an ACCIDENTAL. The sharp works only in the bar in which it is shown and the next bar-line 'rubs it out'. The C in the next bar is thus a natural (unsharpened) one at the first fret on the second string.

There are three new rhythms, related to one another. In bar 4 there is the rhythm ♩. ♩, the first note lasting three times as long as the second. The first complete bar begins with ♩. ♪; again the first note is three times as long as the next. Finally, the rhythm of the very first two notes (which appears many times later) is ♪. ♪, and the first note is three times the length of the second. These are all 'three-to-one' rhythms, the 'one' being a quarter-note, an eighth-note, and a sixteenth-note in turn:

$$♩. \ = \ 3 \times ♩ \quad (♩ + ♩)$$
$$♩. \ = \ 3 \times ♪ \quad (♩ + ♪)$$
$$♪. \ = \ 3 \times ♬ \quad (♪ + ♪)$$

Start by playing the longest of these rhythms slowly and carefully, then gradually play it faster and faster. This will help you to feel what the shorter rhythms are like. You can think of the second one in this way:

♩.　　　♪
one-and-two/and

and when you play it more quickly, you will have the last of these rhythms. This 'dotted rhythm' as musicians sometimes call it, is very typical of cowboy music.

John W. Duarte

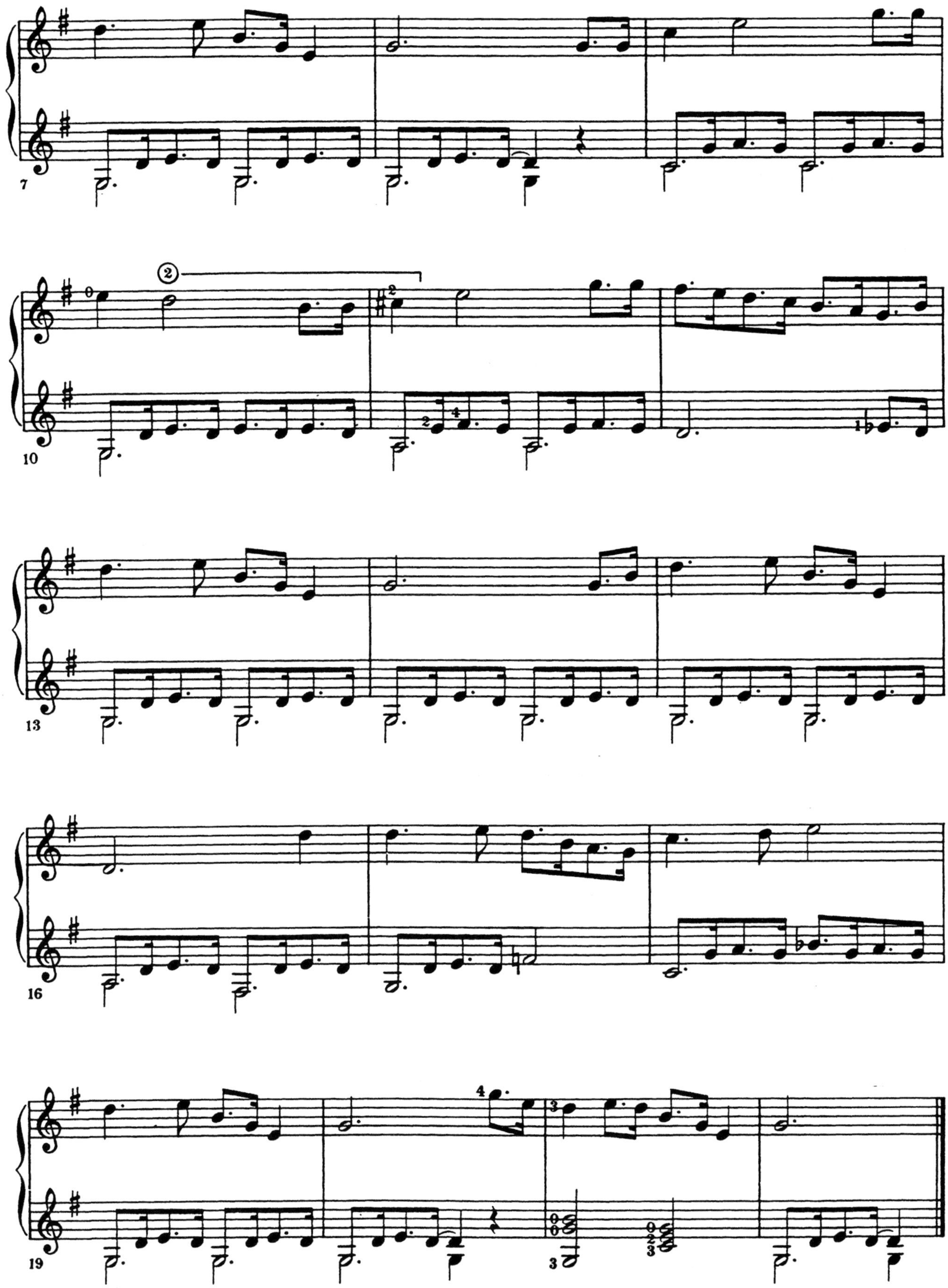

19628

Indians!

What's new?

The key-signature says 'C' but the tune keeps ending on A. Apart from the last 'war-cry' the whole piece ends on A. This time the key is A MINOR, a different key-note and a different *kind* of key; the other two keys you have used have been MAJOR KEYS (though we did not bother to say so at the time) and they sound much brighter and more cheerful than this new minor key. The keys of C major and A minor use the same key-signature (no sharp). Your teacher will explain all this in more detail.

The tune begins *in the middle* of the first bar you play, so be careful to count the rest! The time-signature is a new one, $\frac{2}{4}$, with only two beats in the bar. If you have difficulty, think of it first as having *four* beats, all eighth-notes, like a faster $\frac{4}{4}$; but the tune will make it easier for you so just play it and do not worry.

There are two new notes; both appear more than once, as accidentals:

The sharp on the D and the flat on the A apply only in the bar where they are shown; all other D's and A's are at their natural pitch.

At the very end you have two notes to play at the same time (and very war-like they sound too!). Make sure that your fourth finger is quite upright so that it does not rest against the first string; otherwise it will stop it from sounding and will spoil the effect. Be sure too that you pluck both strings at the same time.

There are plenty of notes to be accented (remember *Ship Ahoy*) and these are marked in the way that you now know.

John W. Duarte

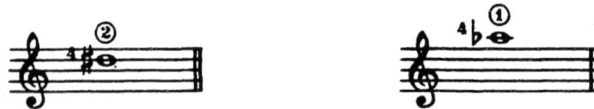

THE
YOUNG PERSONS'
WAY TO THE
GUITAR

by

JOHN W. DUARTE

NOVELLO

FOR THE TEACHER

FOREWORD

The growth of interest in the guitar has been of the most remarkable phenomena in post-war music. It is too well founded and it has lasted too long to support the view that it is probably a 'nine-days-wonder' or some kind of ephemeral 'boom'. The guitar has come to stay as an integral part of the world of music, with its own contribution to make on many fronts. The serious and talented may even study it at many of the principal academies and colleges of music—which do not cater for mere frivolities of popular fashion.

Good teachers of the guitar are still far from plentiful and few are experienced or involved in teaching the young, yet more and more schools are introducing practical music-making through the guitar. The indications are that the movement has still to reach full momentum. As a proportion of good pupils become good teachers the position will improve and may eventually reach a satisfactory balance. There is as yet too widespread a use of the guitar to play simple chords to support singing or, say, a recorder. This may appear to pay rapid dividends but it is an unsound method if it is intended that the pupil shall go further in developing a genuine technique. It does, moreover, scant credit to the guitar as an instrument, and deprives the pupil of the opportunity to enjoy what the guitar has to offer musically. The practice has its uses but it has serious limitations; enjoy it now, pay later.

Very little *simple* guitar music has been written during the last century or more and there is no collection of music and/or exercises intended specifically for teaching the young. This book is a contribution towards the task of making good this lack.

JOHN W. DUARTE
August 1967

INTRODUCTION

A young person lives in his imagination to a greater extent than does the average non-Mitty adult, hence the titles given to much of the music in this book. Though he may not be keen on working at what is essentially an exercise, simply for the good that it will do (under these circumstances 'jam tomorrow' is seldom enough) the young pupil will devote himself more readily to the same exercise if it is more imaginatively titled. To 'climb up and down a ladder' is a more attractive prospect than 'playing scales', even though they may be by definition the same thing, and may therefore be suffered a little more gladly.

A start is made with a few easily accessible notes that enable the pupil to begin making music almost immediately; the wider activity and understanding of a 'scale' can wait until a little later. It is important to capture the interest and co-operation of the pupil as soon as possible. Though there is frequent reference to newly introduced musical terms this is intended not to replace but to reinforce the imparting of musical rudiments by the teacher.*

To minimise the physical problems created by small hands and, equally important, to enable the pupil to make interesting music as soon as possible, initial progress is based on single-line melody. Second parts are provided to give a series of duets that are graded in such a way that the pupil is never faced with too much new enterprise in coming to the next piece.† Interest and involvement are best sustained if each new step is so regulated that obvious 'hard work' is not needed to surmount it.

The presence of a second part played by the teacher (and later by the pupil himself) strengthens confidence and gives important experience in corporate music-making from the outset. The simplest of two-part writing for one guitar poses problems that hinder such immediate involvement in attractive music-making. Duets form the bulk of the music but there are also some easy solo pieces and some exercises to assist physical development of the required kind.

The music does not venture beyond the keys of C, G, and D major, and A minor, but this is not a complete method: it is intended to dovetail on to a standard tutor or course of tuition such as is suitable for adults. As this is a precursor it is not meant to trespass too far into the territory of the standard methods. Just *how* this work is shaded into the following tuition is essentially a problem for each teacher to solve in his own way.

PHYSICAL FACTORS

The correct working of the hands on the guitar requires that the relationship between the sizes of hands and instrument must lie within certain limits. No firm rule could be stated but, as a rough guide, an averagely-built child of nine or ten years should be able to come to terms with a normal full-size guitar.

As many young people may have to use over-large instruments it is even more valuable that the early work should be concentrated on single-line melody with its

---

* The author's *The Guitarist's ABC of Music* (Novello) will be found of great assistance, especially in the teaching of older children.

† The book is intended for those learning the classic guitar but the duets may, with few exceptions, be played on the plectrum guitar. The single-line first parts may also be played on a recorder of suitable range, or any other instrument.

* This is the position at the time of writing but it could of course change at any time.

reduced demands on strength and stretch.

LEFT HAND

The overall size of the left hand is less important than is the ability to separate and use the fingers when they are curved in the normal playing position. Some small hands have a natural ability to spread in this way, compensating for their smallness, while others have to be developed by positive effort. A lack of strength and firmness (the natural pliability of youth) may produce a tendency for the tip-joint of the finger to collapse under the pressure required to hold a string firmly enough on to the fret to give a clear note. Advancing age will usually give greater strength and reduced flexibility and this, together with practice, will eradicate the difficulty; in the meanwhile there are a few things that can be done to help:

1 Emphasize the importance of keeping the tip-joint upright on the fingerboard when applying pressure.

2 Emphasize the importance of placing the finger-tip close behind the fret to obtain a clear note with minimal pressure.

3 Ensure that the pupil's guitar has an action as low as is consistent with the production of good tone and adequate volume.

4 Encourage the carrying out of the 'bend and press' exercise described on page 60.

When the left hand is small in relation to the size of the fingerboard and cannot compensate by an enhanced ability to spread, it may not be possible for the pupil to maintain the correct 'fixed' position of one finger at each fret. Further exercises (and increasing age) will improve the situation but, in the meantime, as it is more important that the pupil should have the pleasure and acquire the confidence of music-making, it is better to tolerate some measure of 'see-sawing' and shifting of the hand as a whole in playing along one string, and not to labour the point unduly. The main emphasis should be on the pleasure of making music, and though a watch must be kept on the development of the correct use of the hands, attention should always be drawn to the fact that a correct action will eventually make it *easier* to play. 'Jam tomorrow' must however always be borne in mind.

RIGHT HAND

There are also difficulties with the right hand when it is small in relation to the size of the instrument. When a small hand is in position to play a chord, for instance in which the thumb plays the sixth string and the third finger the first string, it will be practically impossible to avoid a flatter profile over the back of the hand and the root-joints of the fingers than one would wish (see illustration). The initial concentration on melody means

that the proper use of the right-hand fingers may be cultivated without the need for the thumb to be in position for the lowest strings. The solos in Section Three do of course produce this need and if by this time a good relationship between size of hand and of guitar has not been attained in one way or another, a less-than-ideal position of the hand similar to that illustrated will have to be tolerated for a while. It is however important not to allow this weak and incorrect position to become more firmly entrenched than can be helped.

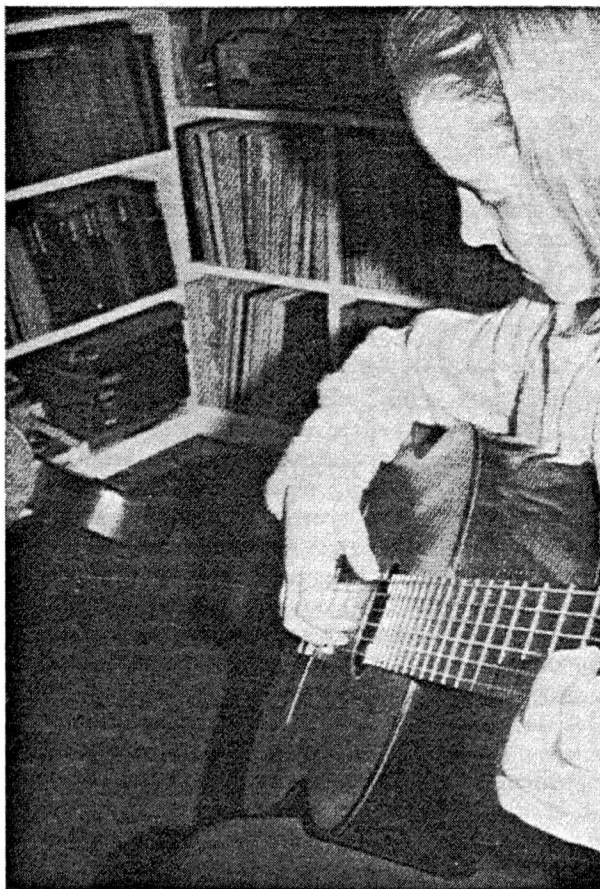

The *apoyando* stroke breeds strength and confidence in a pupil, begin then with the *tirando*.

The most important points are:

1 To encourage the pupil to move the whole finger from its root and not just to 'tweak' the string with the tip-joint.

2 To caution the pupil against 'hooking' the string upwards, a tendency that will be greater if the hand is in a position such as that of Fig. 1. The pupil should be warned of this by exaggerated demonstration and should be encouraged to judge his action by the quality of the sound he produces:

ii

emphasize the importance of nice tone, and warn that if the string is hooked the pupil will, in the long run, not be able to play as loudly!

GENERAL

It is most important for a teacher to be flexible in approach and ready to adapt both requirements and methods to the character and physique of a child. There should be no determination to *impose* anything; instead there should be encouragement to enjoy music and to develop correct technique at the rate that physical development permits, *so that playing will become easier and more adventurous music may be reached.*

No pupil should be either forced or encouraged to persist in practising when the hands ache. This is not only painful and discouraging, it is also physically damaging and can have bad long-term effects. When the aching begins, a short rest or a change in the type of activity is infinitely better than misguided martyrdom; it will also develop strength and endurance much more effectively.

PHYSICAL DEVELOPMENT

Playing a musical instrument is a specialized physical activity, requiring particular abilities that may not be well developed in most people. These abilities may be fostered to a degree that depends upon age and character; children have the greatest potential for physical development, and the earlier they begin, the better.

The physical attributes that are valuable in playing the guitar may be cultivated by simple exercises, though the best way of all is by playing the instrument itself. The main value of separate exercises is that they allow the pupil to concentrate on the main issue, whereas during playing there are other matters that compete for attention, e.g. getting the right notes or using the correct fingers. They do also hasten the development and, with it, the attainment of a comfortable and proper use of the hands.

The exercises as they are given in Section Five of this book are related to the young person's school life by calling them 'P.E.', an activity that most enjoy. A brief period of 'Guitar P.E.' could with benefit become a daily five-minute feature.

Only at a late stage is the half-barré introduced into the music and then only in the second parts. The barré is intensely difficult for most children and it is physically taxing; its use at this early stage has been deliberately avoided. The necessary strength for the less punishing half-barré may be fostered by using the 'bend and press' exercise (page 60) with the finger in the half-barré position.

Many children have soft or weak nails and this prevents their proper use in modern right-hand technique. When this is so the use of flesh alone is often unavoidable; the use of nails should however be tried from time to time until their strength is found to be sufficient. The less time that elapses before the correct 'feel' of nail with a bare minimum of flesh is experienced, the better. The representation of the practice of using flesh only and then nail later as a virtue or a constructive policy is absolute nonsense. A little extra strength may be imparted to weak nails by one or two coats of clear nail varnish; there are also proprietary products on the market for strengthening the nails but they should not be used on young people without prior clearance by a doctor or pharmacist.

Section Four contains exercises to foster the use of the left hand in more extended attitudes, e.g. chords and intervals, and the right hand in the 'arpeggio' position with the thumb engaged on the lower strings.

SECTION ONE

The duets in this section have first parts of progressively increasing difficulty. Suggestions are made later (page iv) for introducing the pupil to second-part playing.

The diatonic ('white') notes up to and including those at the third fret on each string are described as 'ladders'. The second-string ladder is first learned and then used to form a simple tune. This is a short ladder from which the pupil can 'reach' a small amount of music. The ladders on other strings are introduced in order, adding extensions to make a longer ladder from which more and more music may be reached.

The first parts begin with long notes only, and they lead to continuous movement in quarter-notes*. In the course of this the beginnings of confidence are fostered in the pupil by parts that do not follow one another slavishly but are genuinely independent. Also embodied are the graded introduction of movement in eighth-notes, dotted rhythms, different time-signatures, and simple keys (G major, A minor) other than that of C major in which most of these earlier duets are couched.

This book is not a complete tutor but an aid to teachers, who, it is expected, are competent in the elements of the technique of the instrument. It is considered that the 'cleaner' the page the better for the early-stage pupil and, for this reason, right-hand fingerings are not shown; these may be added in pencil or ink at the teacher's discretion.

When a pupil has acquired some measure of facility and confidence in playing the first parts of these duets he or she may be introduced to the invaluable experience of

---

* Fractional terms for note lengths are used, as it is thought that they are more simple for a young person to understand than are the individual names (crotchet, quaver etc.); the latter may be introduced by the teacher as is thought fit. The fractional terms are already common currency on the Continent and in the USA.

iii

playing the second parts. Only the teacher can judge the best point at which to do this with each individual pupil but the following suggestions offer a smooth path and should cover most cases. This book contains the necessary material for many different approaches if teachers prefer to devise their own paths.

With *In the Moonlight* the introduction of all the notes on the first three strings (Ladders A, B, and C) is complete. The notes on the fourth string might be introduced here (Ladder D) so that the better pupil may commence second-part playing at this stage. If this is felt to be too early, the next convenient stage would be after *Conversation*, when all the notes of Ladder D have been learned through the first parts and the duets have fostered a greater degree of independence and strength of individual purpose.

The following progressive path through the second parts places them in approximate order of difficulty and, further, has the advantage that, if the suggestions of the previous paragraph are followed, the pupil will already be familiar with the sound of the pieces through having previously played the first parts

1 *The Cuckoo*
2 *On the Bridge at Avignon*

3 Learn the notes of Ladder E (fifth string)
4 *Our New Car*
5 *Going for a Pony Ride*
6 *My First Tune*
7 *In the Moonlight*
8 *My Bonny*
9 Learn the notes of Ladder F (sixth string)
10 *Bugle and Drum*
11 *Bobby Shaftoe*
12 *Conversation*
13 *O Come, All Ye Faithful*

At this stage all the notes on the lower strings have been introduced and the other second parts (*The Grand Old Duke of York* onwards) may be learned in much the same order as the first parts. Chromatic notes should be identified as required (*Cowboys* onwards). By the end of these duets the pupil will have met the notes at each fret up to and including the fourth on each string; chromatic notes have been described in only one way, e.g. E flat and not D sharp.*

SECTION TWO

The duets in this section carry the pupil progressively up the fingerboard using positioned scale fingerings; their purpose is to give a working knowledge of the diatonic framework covering a fair area of the instrument. A comprehensive knowledge including all chromatic notes is better built up over a longer period.

The progress of the first parts along the fingerboard may be linked with the author's *Guitar Fingerboard Teacher*. A knowledge of pages 7-11 of this booklet covers all the duets in Section One. The duets in the present section correlate as follows:

What Shall We Do With the Drunken Sailor?; *St Paul's Steeple*; *Little Brown Jug*: pages 7-11
Long, Long Ago; *Baa, Baa! Black Sheep*; *Hurry, Hurry, Hurry!*: pages 12-13
The Month of May; *The Mulberry Bush*; *Minuet for Nannerl*; *The Lincolnshire Poacher*: pages 16-17

Amongst the duets in Section One, *Indians!* had a simple dissonance in each part at the end, but only *Cowboys* had a few very simple chords in the second part. The second parts in this section make much more use of chords but they remain simple and without large or punishing stretches. The following gradation of the second parts may be useful in determining the point at which to introduce them to the pupil.

Long, Long Ago Straightforward nut position.

Hurry, Hurry, Hurry! Nut position, busier and chromatic.

St Paul's Steeple Ladder I. Simple, but half-barré used.

Baa, Baa! Black Sheep Ladders G and I. Slightly chromatic

The Month of May Ladder K. Quite easy.

Minuet for Nannerl Ladder K. One chromatic note, more movement.

The Lincolnshire Poacher Ladder J.

The Mulberry Bush Part of Ladder K used in tune. Chords, most of which include only one fingered note.

What Shall We Do With the Drunken Sailor? Chords, very simple. Some single-note passages, very easy.

Little Brown Jug Chords, with one, two, and three fingered notes, but limited stretches. It is advisable to introduce this following the work contained in Section Four, out of which the chords used here arise.

In this section, as in the latter part of Section One, it is advisable to add to the duets usages such as phrasing marks, dynamic markings (very simply introduced in *Bugle and Drum*), and accents. This is better done as 'live' work rather than the interpretation of ready-printed markings; 'worked out' between teacher and pupil. *Involve* the pupil as often and as far as possible.

---

* The use of the author's *Guitar Fingerboard Teacher* (Novello) in conjunction with this book is recommended.

SECTION THREE

These final pieces are solos, presented in roughly increasing order of difficulty; they have been composed for this book, arranged, or merely retitled. Most pupils will play more solos than anything else in the long run and these pieces have been chosen to introduce self-supporting activity painlessly.

Solos emphasize, even at the humblest level, two requirements that have so far been little more than mentioned:

1 Stretches with the left hand, both along and across the fingerboard, to hold down more than one note at a time.

2 The use of the right hand to play more than one note at a time. This includes both the use of the hand in a 'fixed' position in which the top three strings are played with the first three fingers and the lowest three with the thumb, and the playing of *any* two (or more) strings in the most advantageous way.

Section Four includes exercises that help in these directions. *Limbering Up* consists of conventional open-string exercises to foster the use of the hand in a steady position, the simultaneous playing of two or more notes, and the even and independent use of the fingers. The duets in Section Two have some chords in the second parts; it is well to withold these until the open-string exercises are under sufficient control.

The solos abound in thirds, sixths, and tenths and, as these are highly consonant intervals, they are described as 'friends'. It is not essential that the pupil should yet know them by their technical names but it *is* good to focus attention on their character. Other exercises in Section Four help to develop the stretch needed to play these intervals.

No notes accompany these solos in the pupil's book. This is the threshold of normal teaching material and teachers should be able to use this material, at this stage, to make their own approach to their normal (adult) courses. The following notes draw attention to new features in the solos that are worth mentioning to the pupil:

Tyrolean Dance Mostly the closest friends, thirds. Teach how to damp the strings (rests in five bars).

Old Macdonald Had a Farm Less close friends, sixths, but easy to play.

Little Waltz Thirds *and* sixths, a little harder than before.

All My Own Work Bass-and-chord playing, action of right-hand thumb, stretches a little greater than before.

Knights in Armour No new intervals, but the rate of change is faster and action of the right hand slightly different.

The Lass of Richmond Hill Greater variety of intervals, mostly easy. One tenth (under the pause mark) requires two left-hand fingers.

My Minuet Built from tenths; some need two left-hand fingers

Preparing for a Busy Time; Busy Time The solo itself consists of a series of quite easy chords, mostly already familiar, treated as arpeggios (introduce this word) or broken chords. The preparation implants the underlying structure in the pupil's mind so that he can then concentrate on the business of subdividing the chords as necessary. Integral movement from one chord to another is good but can often be smoother if the first note required is secured first; e.g. in bar two, the lower C is required first and the third finger may be placed before the first by a 'short head'.

Russian Folk Song Mostly wide intervals, some octaves. Descending *legato* ('snap') from F to E, three times.

Hurdy-Gurdy Key of D.

Jumbo's Jig Bass-and-chord requiring strong and more agile thumb action.

To and Fro Left-hand pivot finger (e.g. C in bars 1 and 2). Two more descending *legati*. Changes with left-hand fingers while one is in a fixed position (bars 9 and 10).

SECTION FOUR

The exercises in this section are meant to help the pupil to develop stretch in useful ways.

Reach for it! is a preparation for the left-hand stretches needed for thirds, sixths, tenths, and simple chords. In each exercise (or part of one) the pupil keeps his finger firmly in place on the first note until the end of the arrow is reached. At the end his fingers should be in place on both notes so that he can play the interval shown. The two small pieces are similar in that each note marked by an arrow is to be held down until it has to be released to play a lower note on the same string. Throughout *Frère Jacques* the first C is to be held down; likewise the first F in *Funny Little Tune*, at the end of which all three left-hand fingers should be left holding down the chord of F. The hardest and longest stretch is that needed to play the two scales (C and G) without releasing the lowest note in each.

Limbering up is a selection of conventional open-string exercises to introduce the use of the right hand in the position required to 'cover' all six strings. The salient points are to secure the strong and even action of all the digits both in succession and when used together to play (potentially) chords, and to do this without undue movement of the hand as a whole or the adoption of the 'flat' position that can result from this extended attitude of the small hand. Refer back to page iii.

SECTION FIVE

The purpose of this section was stated on page iv and the pupil's book gives a clear account of the exercises themselves and of their objectives. The rôle of the teacher is:

1 To make sure that the pupil is carrying the work out correctly.

2 To advise the time and extent of intensification of the 'bend and press' exercise.

3 To advise the pupil when to move the 'bend and stretch' exercise to lower and wider-spaced frets or to lower strings.

4 To ensure that the pupil does not, in his keenness to progress, over-reach himself to the extent of developing a wrong hand-position.

SECTION SIX

This is a miscellany. There are two ways of making the major scale and a simple sequence more palatable to the young imagination: *Watch the Traffic Lights* and *Countdown and Blast-off*. Finally there are two rounds, playable by two, three, or four guitars, and having entries of the tune with different fingerings. These can be used as best suits the circumstances.

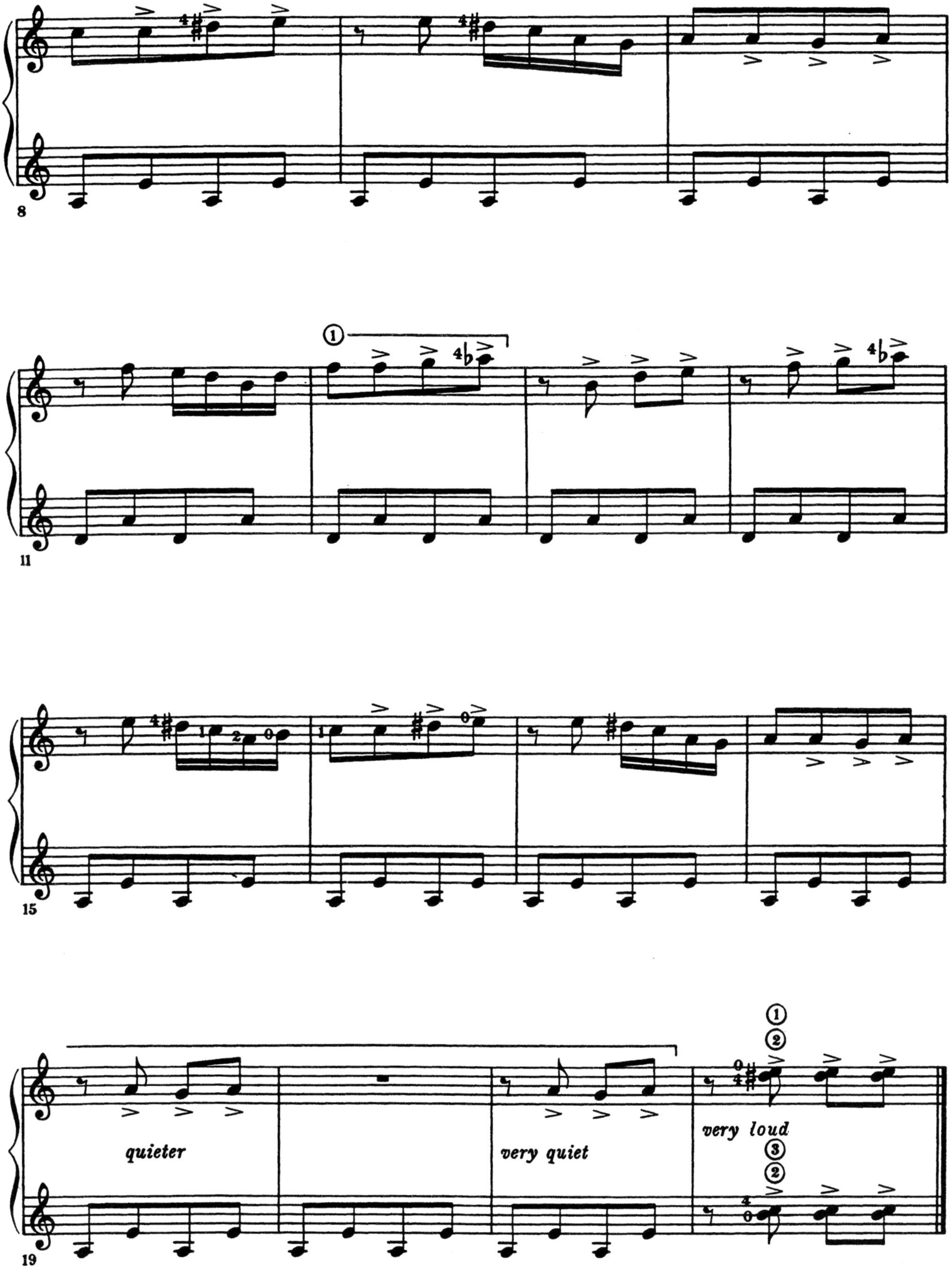
8
11
15
quieter
very quiet
very loud
19

Time to get up!

What's new?

The notes are very familiar, the key is C, the music is quite easy to play, but it is in a new kind of time, 6/8. Each bar has notes (and/or rests) to add up to six eighth-notes and it is easier to think of it as being made up of two halves, counting each as three:

In each bar, the second 'one' is not accented as strongly as the first. The bar should really be counted as having six beats (one, two, three, four, five, six) but it is easier at this moment for you to count two sets of three.

There is a lot of 'conversation' between the two guitars in this piece so be careful to stick to your own part; do not be drawn into listening *too* well to the other!

John W. Duarte

Playtime

Nothing new, but more practice in ⁶/₈ time. This time it is in the key of G.
There are a few dotted half-notes; remember to give them a full count of six
(two threes will do).

John W. Duarte

Now it's Lunchtime!

The first four notes (all half-notes) immediately come again in quarter-notes, and then immediately again in eighth-notes. This makes the piece seem to hurry as it goes along, but do not hurry *too* much! Keep the basic beat steady.

In several bars (bar **6** is the first of them) you have eight eighth-notes but the first is not played; it is only held over (tied) from the bar before. On the first beat you count the 'one' (or, when playing with the other guitar, wait for the second guitar to 'count' it for you by playing its note) and then begin playing your eighth-notes on the first 'and':

one / and / two / and / three / and / four / and
(held) play-----------------------------------

Most of this piece is 'conversational' so stick to your own story!

John W. Duarte

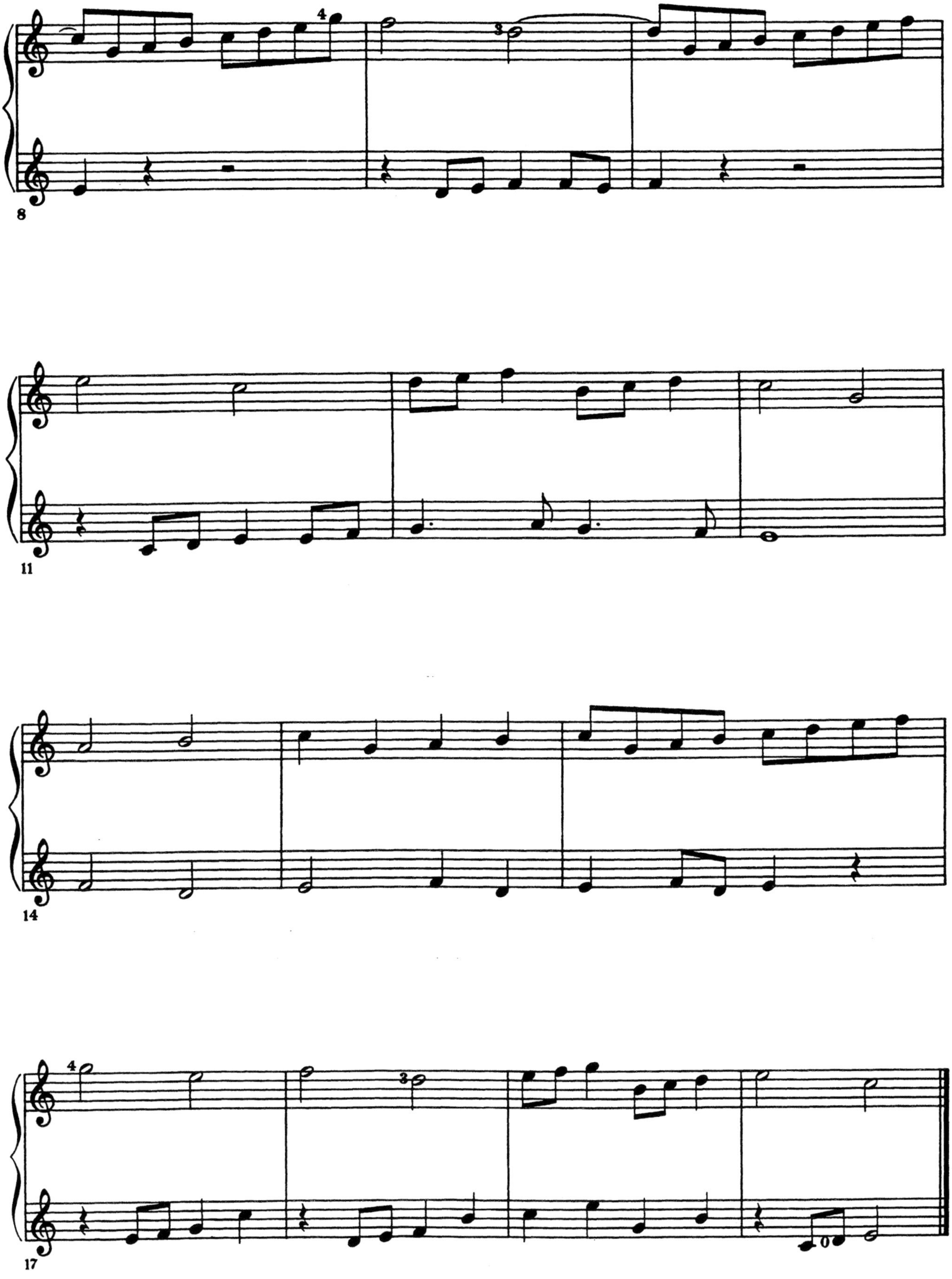
4
3
8
11
14
4
3
17
0

Bedtime

What's new?

There is one new note, which appears as an accidental only:

Don't forget that although accidentals reign for the length of the bar in which they are shown, they are deposed at the end of the bar: all other G's are thus natural. There are also several F sharps which appear as accidentals, but these are not new; you have had this note before in pieces in the key of G but not, of course, as accidentals.

The rhythm with which the piece begins is ♩. ♪♪ . The first two notes are to a dotted rhythm (revise *Cowboys* if this has slipped your memory). As a guide, the first bar is played to the same rhythm as the well-known *Rock-a-bye Baby*.

Again your part is independent of the other guitar. You should be used to this by now and you will not need nursing through your parts as you did when you began. Be especially careful to count the quarter-note rest in the bar immediately before the last; notice how you answer the second guitar, as though you both said 'goodnight'!

John W. Duarte

4

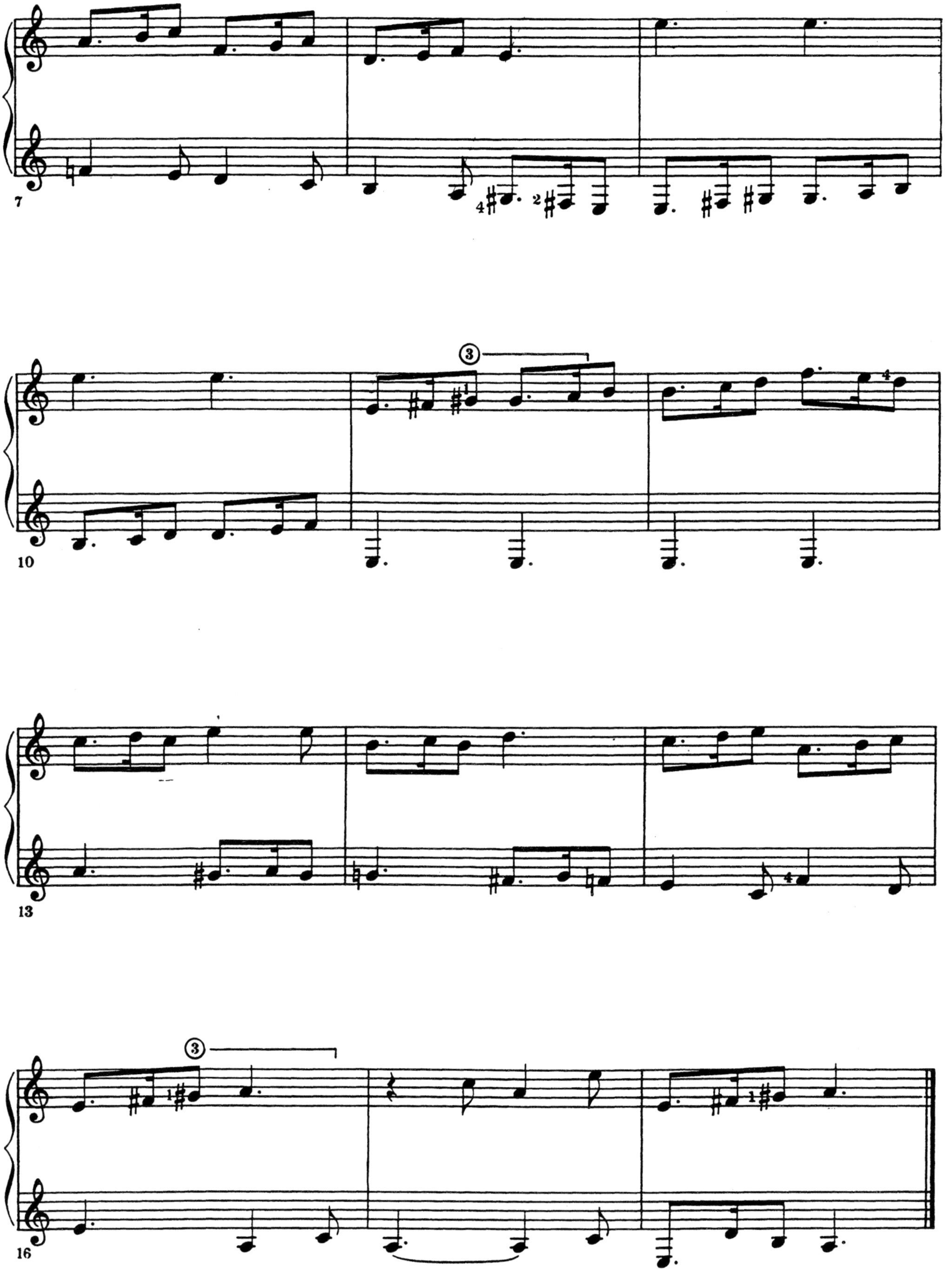
7
10
13
16

Section Two

GOING UP!

All the pieces in the first section were in the NUT POSITION. This means that the notes were those nearest the nut (see the diagram on page V) and you have used a lot of OPEN STRINGS— a string is 'open' when it is not held down by a left-hand finger. In these next pieces you will not immediately give up the open strings but you will move steadily away from the nut and further up the fingerboard— nearer to the body of the guitar.

You will first learn and then use higher ladders, to reach even more music. Of course you could go on playing near the nut as you have been doing, just reaching along the first string for the highest notes. This would be silly! You would have to hop up and down the fingerboard and sometimes you would surely find your fingers in the wrong places. It is better to learn new, higher ladders than to play at this risky game. By using the higher ladders you will be able to move *across* the fingerboard instead of up and down. A shorter ladder on a higher level is far better than a long, wobbly one resting on the ground.

What shall we do with the Drunken Sailor?

What's new?

This piece does not use a higher ladder but it does introduce you gently to the idea of moving up the fingerboard. In bar 6 you use the first finger at the *second* and the rest in order, so that you reach as far as the fifth fret, note A, with your little finger.

In bar 5 you do not use any finger of your left hand; whilst the hand is free you move it one fret higher than usual, ready to play F sharp with your index finger.

In bar 7 you move your hand back to its original position whilst you play the second note (E), which leaves the hand free for a moment.

The same things happen again later:

Bar 13: hand is free, move up one fret.

Bar 14: use your hand one fret higher than usual.

Bar 15: second note leaves your hand free to move back to the usual position.

Higher Ladders

19628

St. Paul's Steeple

What's new?

There are no new (high) notes to play; what is new is the place in which you finger some of those you already know. To play this piece you need to know Ladder G; this is the scale of C played a little higher up the fingerboard than you have met it before.

As in *What shall we do with the Drunken Sailor?* you use your first finger at the *second* fret and the others, in turn, one fret higher too.

At the very end, try to let all the last three notes (G, E and C) ring together: don't lift your first finger from the E when you play the final C.

Many of the notes are now being played on a lower string than before and this gives them a different, fuller, tone than before.

40

Little Brown Jug

What's new?

Ladder G is extended by two notes to give Ladder H.

In bar **8** the note G is played on the third string (open) and not on the fourth string as in Ladder G. This is to avoid your having to lift your fourth finger from one string to the other and back again! The same applies to the last bar of the whole piece. For the same reason the G which begins bar **9** is played on the open G string.

Long Long Ago

What's new?

Before playing this you must learn the notes of Ladder I. This is further along the fingerboard than you have been before but the frets are closer together and this makes it a little easier.

One note only is played outside Ladder I, this is the G at the end of bars 9 and 11. You could play this with your first finger at the fifth fret on the fourth string, but it is not quite as easy to reach there if your hand is small.

At the end of the page there is the instruction *D. C. al Fine*. This means that you play the whole page, leaving out the bar marked ⌐2⎤, then go back to the beginning and play, leaving out the bar marked ⌐1⎤, until you come to the place marked *Fine* and here you stop. Over the last note there is also a sign like a half-circle with a dot and it tells you to pause on the note, and not just to play it as a half-note.

19628

Baa, Baa Black Sheep

What's new?

You play the tune once in Ladder I and then the second guitar plays it lower down whilst you follow him one bar later. What you do is almost but not quite in canon. If you have forgotten what a canon is, turn back to *Follow Me* on page **24**

No *D. C. al Fine* is marked, but if you like you can go back to the beginning and repeat the first eight bars in which you have the tune high up. I know you had this tune earlier on! This time, though, it is in a different key, a higher position, and it is arranged differently. Play the two settings one after another and compare them.

Hurry, Hurry, Hurry!

What's new?

There is nothing entirely new but this piece leaves you less time to 'breathe' than any other so far. It is full of eighth-notes; a lot of them are the same note repeated several times, giving you plenty of practice with your alternate right-hand fingers. In several places you have to change from one string to the next in the middle of a run of eighth-notes; watch this carefully, it is tricky, especially where you have to change from, say, the first string to the second. It is easier to let your hand drop towards the ground than it is to lift it!

The title means that the piece should be played briskly, but do not hurry it so much that you cannot play it properly with every note sounding clearly. Remember, 'more haste, less speed'!

John W. Duarte

The Month of May

What's new?

For this tune you need to know the notes of Ladder J– which is in fact a scale of G in the highest position you have yet reached on the guitar.

In three places there are DOUBLE BARS WITH REPEATS, in the middle of bars 4, 12, and 16. They have two dots next to them; these are repeat signs. A repeat sign sends you back, once only, either to the beginning of the piece or to the previous repeat sign.

Like *Baa, Baa Black Sheep,* the tune is played the second time by the other guitar whilst you play another part. This time your part makes a nice little tune in itself, without imitating the original tune; your part is called a COUN-TER-MELODY– a melody that is played against the original one. The counter-melody takes you further down Ladder J than does the tune itself.

At the beginning of bar 5, why do you play the note A with your *third* finger? Think about it, and ask your teacher for the answer if you do not know!

Practically all the second part of this piece is written with the notes from Ladder K; this is a scale of G closer to the nut but not using any open strings. You will have to learn this new ladder when you play the second part of this duet.

19628

The Mulberry Bush

The tune and most of the counter-melody in the second section (when the second guitar has the tune) use the notes of Ladder J.

What's new?

One new note in the first part: C sharp at the ninth fret.

The second part has some chords but in most of these only one string is fingered by the left hand. If you are playing the second part, hold down the bottom G all through bars 1, 2, 5, 6, and 8, and try to hold on to the top D in bar 4, for as long as it is marked. Notice that this D is tied: two notes are written but only the first is struck. The tune in the second section uses many but not all the notes of Ladder K.

Minuet for Nannerl

This is one of many pieces written by the great composer Wolfgang Amadeus Mozart (what a lovely name!) who lived from 1756 to 1791, for his sister, Nannerl, of whom he was very fond.

What's new?

There is nothing completely new, but a few things are worth noting.

1 Though you should have learned the whole of Ladder J by now, this is the first time you have needed the lowest notes when playing a piece.

2 Remember the two little 'dashes' at the end of bar 12: they tell you to 'take a quick breath'.

3 You have repeat marks again. The first takes you back to the beginning, the second takes you back to the previous double bar.

4 The second part mostly uses the notes of Ladder K. There is also a C sharp — not a new note, but played, this time, with the first finger.

W. A. Mozart

The Lincolnshire Poacher

All the notes in *both* parts are drawn from Ladder J.

What's new?

In the *middle* of bar **12** there is a double bar with a repeat mark after it. You play right through this (the repeat mark comes *after* the double bar) and up to and including the bar that has a repeat mark at its end (it is in fact only a half-bar) and a bracket, with a number 1, over it. These bars between the repeat marks are of course played twice *but* the second time you play them, you do not play the half-bar under this bracket; you play that which is under the *second* bracket instead, to finish. These are called FIRST and SECOND TIME BARS, and they are placed at the end of a repeated passage when you are to play a different ending each time.

Section Three
SOLO FLIGHTS

Now that you know your way around the guitar a little better you can play some solo pieces, which need no accompaniment from anyone else. They have their own accompaniment built into them. This means that very often you have to play a note in the tune, at the same time as you play an accompanying note either higher or lower than the tune. There are very many possible combinations of two notes, but we will give our attention mainly to the most important of them; these pairs of notes sound very agreeable together and we can look on them as two friends. As well as these solo pieces you will meet and learn to play these various musical friends; in their turn they will help you with the solos in this book.

When you have finished with this book you will go on to new adventures—more difficult pieces, more exciting music; these adventures could last for the rest of your life. No matter how long you may play the guitar you will find these pairs of notes to be good friends, not only to one another but to you too.

Meeting some good friends

These are *close* friends

These live a long way apart, but they are still good friends

And they can be even friendlier

Tyrolean Dance

Josef Küffner

Old Macdonald Had a Farm

Little Waltz

Mauro Giuliani

All My Own Work

John W. Duarte

Knights in Armour

Josef Küffner

The Lass of Richmond Hill

My Minuet

John W. Duarte

Preparing for a Busy Time

19628

Busy Time

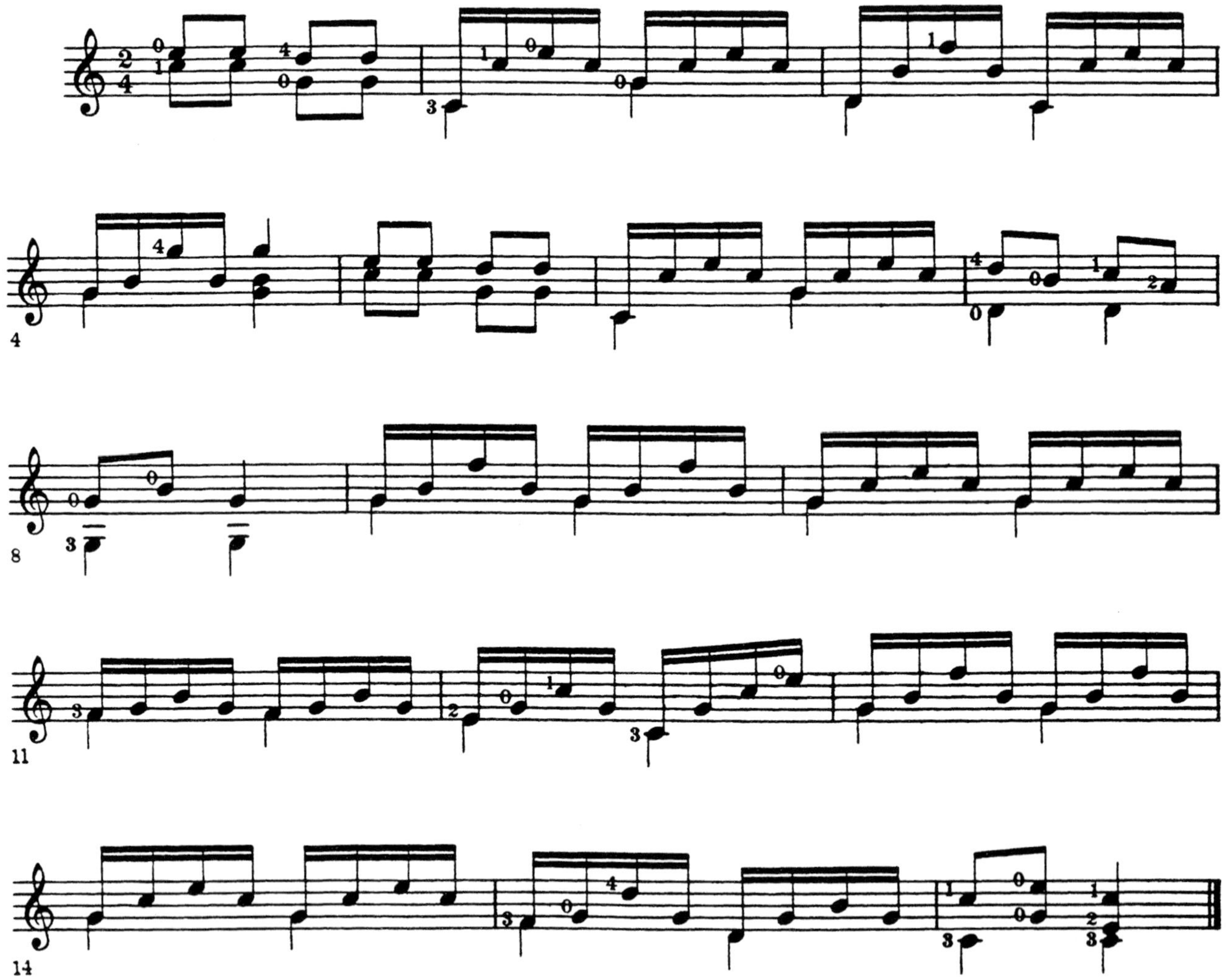

Russian Folk-song

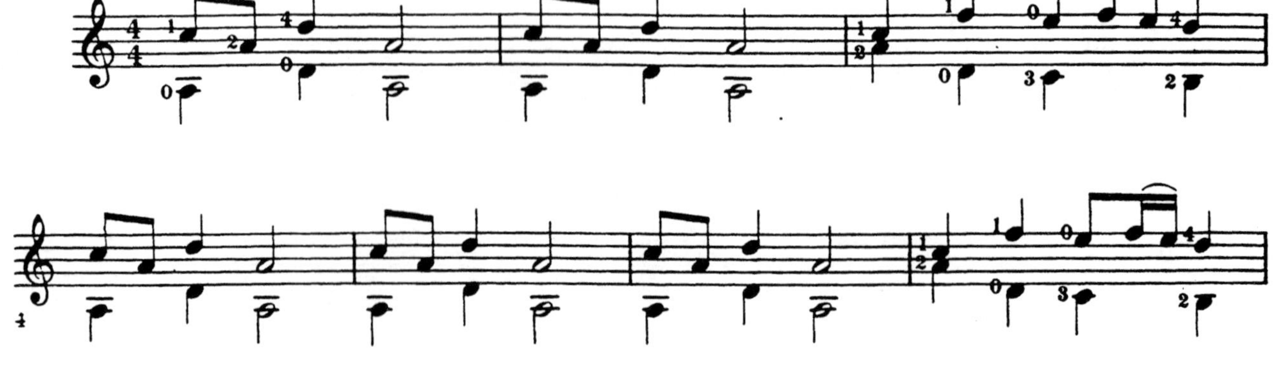

Hurdy-Gurdy

John W. Duarte

Jumbo's Jig

John W. Duarte

With a loud thumb!

To and Fro

John W. Duarte

Section Four
REACH FOR IT!

The activities in this part of the book will help you to develop the stretch and reach that you will need to play the solos in Section Three. You will have to stretch across the strings with your right hand and across the fingerboard with your left.

Your teacher will show you exactly what to do but the important thing to remember is that in *Holding on*, the first note in each line has an arrow starting from it; you must hold this note down right to the end of the arrow without once letting it go. At the end of the line you play the pair of notes *together*; what goes before prepares you for the stretch that you need for this. You will meet these stretches many times in your guitar playing from now on.

In playing the activities in *Limbering up*, keep your right hand as steady as possible, confining the movement as much as possible to your fingers and not moving your whole hand about.

Holding on

Frère Jacques

Funny Little Tune

John W. Duarte

Limbering up

Section Five

GUITAR P.E.

Probably you already enjoy P.E. (physical exercise) at school; now you can add Guitar P.E. These simple exercises can be done at any time and they will gradually make it easier for you to play the guitar.

Bend and press

Bend the fingers of your left hand into the correct curve for playing.

Press each finger in turn, separately, on to the fingerboard at *any* fret.

Keep up the pressure for a count of two and then relax it.

Do this six times with each finger. As your strength increases you can increase the number of times you press, or the length of time you keep up the pressure (a longer count).

Stretch and press

Hold down the first string at the ninth fret with the first finger of your left hand.

Leave your first finger in place and now press your second finger down at the tenth fret.

Leave both fingers pressed down and add the third finger at the eleventh fret; you now have three fingers pressed down at adjoining frets.

Finally, press down the string at the twelfth fret with the fourth finger so that all four fingers now press the string down.

You must keep each finger in place until the whole exercise is finished. If you let go with the first finger, for instance, when you add the third finger, the exercise will be spoiled.

When you can do this comfortably you can repeat it on lower strings at the same frets, and on the first string, beginning at lower frets, which, being larger, make you spread your fingers more. Your teacher will tell you where and when to do this when the time is right.

'Quick March' and 'At the Double'

Bend the fingers of your right hand into the correct curve for playing.

Now hold your hand over a table or other flat surface with the palm downwards. Rest your wrist on the back of your *left* hand to steady it and hold it up.

Tap on the table with your first and second fingers, one after the other, like marching with these fingers as legs. Do it firmly and positively.

Be sure to move your fingers from the place where they join on to the rest of your hand. Don't just move the tip joints. The action should be like that you use when you play the strings of the guitar.

Continue 'marching' until your fingers feel a little tired, *then stop*.

To move 'at the double', alternate your fingers more quickly but still steadily and with regular steps. The better you get, the faster you will be able to run without stumbling.

Practice marching and running with your second and third fingers also, in the same way.

Section Six
ODDS FOR THE END

Watch the Traffic Lights

John W. Duarte

Count-down

John W. Duarte

Blast-off

London's Burning

My Dame Hath a Lame Tame Crane

19628

Printed and bound in the United Kingdom by Page Bros (Norwich) Ltd

4/04 (50998)

MUSIC FOR GUITAR

SOLO

ANONYMOUS
trans Rooley
SIX ANONYMOUS LUTE SOLOS

BACH, J S
arr Duarte
FOURTH CELLO SUITE

CROUCHER, Terence
ELEGY

DUARTE, John
ENGLISH SUITE
SIX EASY PICTURES
VARIATIONS ON A CATALAN FOLK
SONG

VARIOUS
arr Duarte
CAROLS FOR GUITAR SOLO
FORTY COMMUNITY SONGS
SIXTEEN ENGLISH FOLK SONGS
THREE ENGLISH FOLK SONGS

DUET

ANONYMOUS
arr Duarte
MORE OF THESE ANON

BACH, J S
arr Duarte
BACH AT THE BEGINNING

DUARTE, John
SIX FRIENDSHIPS FOR TWO
GUITARS

HANDEL, G F
arr Biberian
CHACONNE IN G WITH TWENTY-ONE
VARIATIONS

HANDEL, G F
arr Duarte
HANDEL'S TURN

TRIO

GASTOLDI, Giovanni
arr Duarte
SIX BALLETS

QUARTET

BIBERIAN, Gilberian
SUITE FOR GUITAR QUARTET

DOWLAND, John
arr Biberian
THREE DANCES

DUARTE, John
LITTLE SUITE

PRAETORIUS, Michael
arr Duarte
FOUR FRENCH DANCES

Novello

608 (90)